New Concepts in
Digital Reference

Synthesis Lectures on Information Concepts, Retrieval, and Services

Editor
Gary Marchionini, *University of North Carolina, Chapel Hill*

New Concepts in Digital Reference
R. David Lankes

ISBN: 978-3-031-01131-3   print
ISBN: 978-3-031-02259-3   ebook

DOI: 10.1007/978-3-031-02259-3

A Publication in the Springer series

SYNTHESIS LECTURES ON INFORMATION CONCEPTS, RETRIEVAL, AND SERVICES # 1

Lecture #1

Series Editor: Gary Marchionini, University of North Carolina, Chapel Hill

Series ISSN Pending

New Concepts in Digital Reference

R. David Lankes

School of Information Studies, Syracuse University

SYNTHESIS LECTURES ON INFORMATION CONCEPTS, RETRIEVAL, AND SERVICES # 1

ABSTRACT

Let us start with a simple scenario: a man asks a woman "how high is Mount Everest?" The woman replies "29,029 feet." Nothing could be simpler. Now let us suppose that rather than standing in a room, or sitting on a bus, the man is at his desk and the woman is 300 miles away with the conversation taking place using e-mail. Still simple? Certainly—it happens every day. So why all the bother about digital (virtual, electronic, chat, etc.) reference?

If the man is a pilot flying over Mount Everest, the answer matters. If you are a lawyer going to court, the identity of the woman is very important. Also, if you ever want to find the answer again, how that transaction took place matters a lot.

Digital reference is a deceptively simple concept on its face: "the incorporation of human expertise into the information system." This lecture seeks to explore the question of how human expertise is incorporated into a variety of information systems, from libraries, to digital libraries, to information retrieval engines, to knowledge bases. What we learn through this endeavor, begun primarily in the library context, is that the models, methods, standards, and experiments in digital reference have wide applicability. We also catch a glimpse of an unfolding future in which ubiquitous computing makes the identification, interaction, and capture of expertise increasingly important. It is a future that is much more complex than we had anticipated. It is a future in which documents and artifacts are less important than the contexts of their creation and use.

KEYWORDS

virtual reference, reference, conversation theory, participatory librarianship

Contents

C H A P T E R   1

Introduction

Knowledge is created through conversation. Through an interchange with another person, an organization, even with yourself, you "know." Knowing is a product of the language exchanged, the agreements reached between the conversants, and the structure of those agreements in your memory over time.

This may seem like an odd way to start an exploration of digital reference and its relation to digital libraries. Yet, it is this central premise of how we learn that defines not only the need for reference, but also its central importance to the future of digital libraries. It is through this seemingly simple statement—knowledge is created through conversation—that we will explore what has been called online reference, virtual reference, digital reference, and a whole host of other titles.

Here is how I shall tackle this topic. First, let us get the business of terms and definitions out of the way. Then, let us explore the underlying concepts behind conversations in digital libraries. Lastly, let us look at the practicalities of virtual reference and explore some new services around digital reference. Let me be clear at the outset that this is not a treatise covering the whole of reference, including its historical roots. Neither does this lecture attempt to cover the full aspects of digital reference practice in detail. There are plenty of other sources for this kind of detailed reflection on praxis. Not only would another treatment on the realities of today's digital reference world seem redundant, but it would also be unhelpful.

It is implied throughout this document that something new is needed to push the art and science of reference forward. The explosion of reference development throughout the beginning of the 21st century is breathtaking. From concept and experiments in the 1990s to mainstay of library service today, it is clear that digital reference has accomplished a great deal. However, the momentum of functions, applications, and conceptual foundations seems to be ebbing. The new spark that will advance human mediated information seeking will not come from another application or a new interface. Rather, the future evolution of reference relies on deeper understandings of communication and the increasingly social nature of knowledge in the world of ubiquitous connection. Some of the work is captured within this lecture, but much more is needed.

· · · ·

CHAPTER 2

Defining Reference in a Digital Age

At the outset, let me say that I consider the phrases "virtual reference" and "digital reference" to be synonymous. I take some blame for the coining of the phrase digital reference, and did so to better show the link between digital reference and digital libraries. The field of librarianship, with a few notable examples, more often uses the term virtual reference in much the same way they used virtual library before the preponderance of the phrase digital library. While I think the terminology wars are lost, and irrelevant, I keep the modifier "digital" in order to once again make explicit the link between reference and the digital library.

There are several definitions of digital or virtual reference. The American Library Association's Reference & User Services Association (RUSA, 2004) defines it as:

> Virtual reference is reference service initiated electronically, often in real-time, where patrons employ computers or other Internet technology to communicate with reference staff, without being physically present. Communication channels used frequently in virtual reference include chat, videoconferencing, Voice over IP, co-browsing, e-mail, and instant messaging.

OCLC (2007) defines it as "Using computer and communications technology to provide reference service to patrons anytime and anywhere." The problem with these definitions is that they rely upon an understanding of "reference," as defined in libraries. The world of answering questions online is much larger than libraries, as we shall see.

The definition we shall use for this lecture comes from the Digital Reference Research Agenda (Lankes et al., 2003):

> The use of human intermediation to answer questions in a digital environment.

A definition is necessary but insufficient. A definition can, at best, identify a field or practice. It does not include the analysis necessary to define the shape and direction of the field. Any domain of inquiry is predicated on a central question. As stated by Lankes et al. (2003):

> The central driving question provides boundaries for the unique nature of a discipline and situates the domain in the realm of other streams of exploration. In the specific case of digital reference, the central question must center on why digital reference is different from traditional library-based reference research and from digital library research. It must also, of course, define how digital reference is related to these domains as well as to information retrieval, and computer mediated communication. The digital reference research agenda described in this article poses the central question in digital reference as:
>
> *How can human expertise be incorporated effectively and efficiently into information systems to answer information seekers' questions?*
>
> This central driving question comes with several components and assumptions that form the basic framework of the research agenda.

It is this broad definition and this central question that drive this lecture and much of the research and ideas held within.

What emerges from the definition and driving question is a framework that is translated into a specific agenda. This framework (seen in Figure 2.1) consists of a series of lenses or approaches to the central question of incorporating human expertise into the digital library (such as "evaluation"—how does one determine if human expertise has been incorporated efficiently and effectively). The framework also has question components (such as what is meant by "questions" and "answers") and a set of assumptions to be tested (such as "is human expertise useful to incorporate into a system").

This framework can be represented in a matrix form and filled in with specific research questions:

The matrix can also be used to track what has been investigated and what remains to be looked at. Table 2.1 represents the author's perspective on well-researched areas and those needing more investigation or at the other extreme.

So, for example, there has been a great deal of research into evaluation of efficiency and effectiveness of digital reference (see McClure et al., 2002; Pomerantz et al., 2008; Mon, 2006; Carter & Janes, 2000; Kaske & Arnold, 2005; Ruppel & Fagen, 2005; Ward & Lee, 2004 for examples).

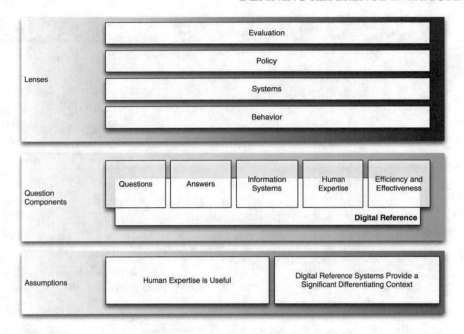

FIGURE 2.1: The structure of the digital reference research agenda.

TABLE 2.1: Author's perspective on well-researched areas and those needing more investigation or at the other extreme

	POLICY	SYSTEMS	EVALUATION	BEHAVIOR
Human expertise	Low	Medium	Medium	Low
Efficiency and effectiveness	High	Low	High	Low
Information systems	Medium	High	High	High
Questions	High	Medium	Low	Medium
Answers	Medium	Medium	Medium	Medium

High, high coverage (well-researched areas); low, little available research (needs more investigation).

	POLICY	SYSTEMS	EVALUATION	BEHAVIOR
Human expertise	What are the necessary staffing levels, expertise, and training?	How is human output incorporated into system components (such as a knowledgebase)?	What are the perceived benefits of human mediation (familiarity of human voice: content expertise: instruction)?	Do users ask questions differently when they know a human intermediary is involved?
Efficiency and effectiveness	What limits should be placed on a service and how are they determined?	What level of automation can be used in digital reference?	What metrics are needed to determine cost/value in digital reference? Does knowledge of cost in digital reference effect behavior?	Does knowledge of cost in digital reference affect behavior?
Information systems	How can digital reference systems be constructed to protect individual privacy and licensing while achieving maximum benefit for an intended community?	What are the required components of a digital reference system?	What are appropriate performance metrics for system evaluation?	How do experts and users interact in a digital reference system?
Questions	How do services determine out-of-bound questions?	What systems work best as an interface to get at user questions?	Have questions qualitatively changed over time in digital reference (gotten more difficult)?	What digital aids can be used to aid users to construct questions?
Answers	What policies do or should bind service responses (copyright)?	Can knowledgebases be better used to provide answers to some types of questions?	How do you determine "right" and "wrong" answers?	What are the necessary components of an answer needed to meet a user's information need?

Marie Radford's (2001) work on the reference interview and reference encountering has lead to a substantial body of knowledge in the area of "How do experts and users interact in a digital reference system?" This digital reference encountering research continues a long line of research into the reference interview that includes seminal work by Taylor (1968) and Dervin (1986). There is also a healthy literature in international issues in digital reference (see Shachaf et al., 2007; Shachaf & Horowitz, 2006). At the same time, little has been done to conduct longitudinal research in the questions users ask [though Miwa (2000) has made a good start in her dissertation work].

The overall impression from Table 2.1 is that much is actually known about digital reference, yet there remains much work to be done. What Table 2.1 does not show is that much of the foundational work was conducted on an existing model of reference. Little has been done to envision new ways to break out of a reference desk approach. What is a "reference desk" approach? A great deal of what has been formally studied in reference online has focused on what libraries are doing. Reference in libraries has been developed over nearly a century, and almost all of it focuses on a physical desk.

To illustrate this desk-centric approach, let us say that a user has a question. Let us call him Riley. How will Riley get his answer at his library (in this example, the actual type of library is irrelevant)? Riley is first expected to go to the library. Once within the library, he is expected to find and approach a reference desk. This desk is most likely big, and it is often elevated. Once at the desk, he needs to attract the attention of a reference librarian and, possibly, wait in line. He is then expected to go into a reference interview, often short, and data shows, often little more than Riley stating his question. What Riley does not know is that the reference librarian has been taught that the most important question to ask Riley is why he needs this information—and that the reference librarian should never phrase the question as "why do you need this information" so as to protect Riley's privacy and not insult him. The librarian then takes Riley's question and points him to a set of resources, physical and digital, that should have relevant information (not necessarily the answer) that Riley seeks. What is amazing about this interaction is that there is a great chance Riley will be highly satisfied with the interaction, and there is a 45% chance he received the wrong answer (Hernon & McClure, 1987).

It should also be obvious that there are many environmental conditions that can get in the way of Riley even asking the question. There is a power relationship occurring (Riley had to go to the library). There are physical barriers (the desk). There is also the fact that Riley had to stop any activities he was working on as part of getting an answer, to go to the librarian.

Rather than limit this analysis to libraries, there are plenty of barriers to question-asking put in place by help desks and customer service centers that can be discussed. We all have been stuck in a less than helpful phone tree before (press 1 to do this, press 2 to do this...). In fact, many companies, seeing reference-like activities as inherently human, and thus inherently expensive, actively dissuade users from the service. If you wish to book a flight on an airline today, you get charged a booking fee of $25 or so if you call and talk to a ticketing agent, while there is no fee for doing it yourself online. Try and find a phone number on the Amazon web site.

One very interesting study was of interactions in high school classrooms. It noted that girls do not ask as many questions as boys. These studies showed that not only did such inhibited question asking behavior lead to reduced teacher–student interaction, it had very real consequences in later performance. Classroom environment, gender discrimination, power issues, and curriculum, it seems, conspire to keep girls from asking questions, which in turn leads to poor performance. We can hypothesize that such inhibitions on asking question are environmental, not biological, when you look at the gender of users in homework help and online reference services geared toward K-12. Here, the data shows that girls actually outnumber boys in asking questions.

2.1   SO WHY CARE ABOUT QUESTIONS?

So why care about all of this question asking? Would it not be better to simply treat them as queries and draw upon the long tradition of information retrieval and information seeking to determine regularities in queries and automate the process as much as possible? There certainly has been a great deal of effort in eliminating just this sort of human intermediation in almost all sectors of the economy, including in the digital library world.

In 2002, Bill Arms, principal investigator on the National Science Digital Library project, made a presentation to OCLC. Arms (2002) included the slide in Figure 2.2. This slide makes

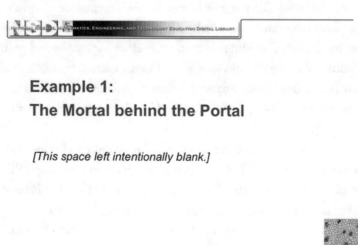

FIGURE 2.2: Slide from Bill Arm's presentation to OCLC.

sense if you consider that people cost more money than computers. It makes even more sense if you define a digital library as a collection of document-like objects. If you are dealing with often-static documents and some system of access, one can assume that there is a finite number ways of seeking and organizing the digital library collection. Once you have identified them (or at least the predominant ones) it should be an achievable task to eliminate questions of access.

This fixation on automation in digital libraries is easy to understand when put in the document-centric context. After all, there is a huge and growing corpus of documents for inclusion in digital libraries. As work in the area of metadata shows, human cataloging of materials is a losing game. There must be some form of automation if you have a collection of any size. Many have extended this logic to reference activities as well. Just as we automated access to materials, can we not also automate the process of resolving questions that arise from access? This, of course, completely misses the point that access to materials is intended for some sort of learning activity that will lead to more questions.

However, what if we did not look at a digital library as a collection of document-like objects? After all, if Web 2.0 has shown us anything, the real action is in services. Is MySpace a repository of documents? Is Facebook? Even in something like Flickr there is something more interesting going on than a simple collection of images. The answer to "why care about questions" is because if you look at how people ask questions—how they come to know something—not only do you understand the need for reference in a digital library, you start to see the way forward to reinventing the entire concept of a digital library.

2.2   THE WORD GAME

I stated before that the way forward in digital reference is through communications. Rather than focusing on how software allows us to answer questions online, we need to step back and understand how people ask them in the first place. To do that, I want to walk you through a seemingly trivial game. It is a game intended to demonstrate how we think. I am going to give you a word, and you define the word. OK, first word:

Formula

When I say the word formula, what do you think about? A chemical combination? A mathematical expression? How about something you feed to a baby? OK, what if I show you the picture in Figure 2.3? How about now? Did it change? Let us try another one:

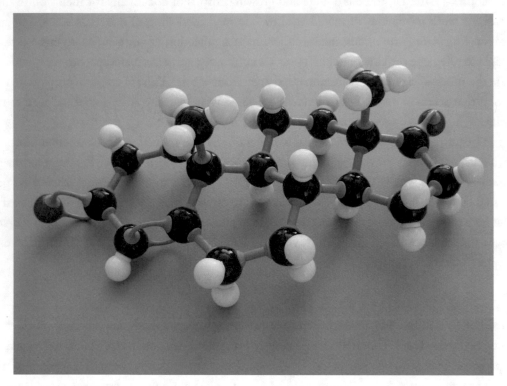

FIGURE 2.3: Formula.

Light

Did you think about illumination? Setting something ablaze? The opposite of heavy? Maybe none of these. Now, what if I show you the picture in Figure 2.4? How about now? What is going on? What is going on is that you understand all of these meanings of the word light or formula, and you understand them as relationships. Since you encounter them often, you actually have a lot of relationships with these words. In fact, they are so common that the words themselves mean very little, but your brain is trying to do what a brain does—seek meaning. It does this by anticipating, or guessing at a relationship until some piece of confirming, or disproving piece of data comes along. In this case, the confirming bit of context is the picture. It is not until a context is introduced that your mind snaps to a relationship that you already know.

These two cases (light and formula) are words with a lot of relationships. However, some terms have very few. Take this next example:

FIGURE 2.4: Light.

OMG!

I am going to go ahead and guess you did not think of "Object Management Group" or the "Omnicom Media Group." I am going to guess you thought of "Oh My God!" Not only are there few relationships with this acronym, but the relationship that does exist in your mind is so strong you can actually add the context yourself. If I had you guess at a picture I might put up, Figure 2.5 probably would not surprise you.

FIGURE 2.5: OMG.

Indeed, many of the relationships of words, pictures, and ideas that we hold in our head, in a sort of web of ideas, are increasingly socially derived. That is, we come to understand things as communal relationships that are defined not as a single person, but as a group. Take that picture of the light bulb in Figure 2.4. In 10 years or so, it will actually mean very little because, increasingly, we as a society are pressured to think about light bulbs looking like Figure 2.6.

Some of us may still remember when CFCs were not compact fluorescents but an ozone-destroying gas that had to be eliminated from the environment. The real power of the brain comes in its ability to scaffold ideas, terms, and concepts and combine them together. For example, what happens when you combine:

FIGURE 2.6: Light bulb.

forumula+light+OMG?

How about Figure 2.7?

This combination of concepts is also socially derived. For example, try this combination:

FIGURE 2.7: Formula+light+OMG. Image courtesy fotosearch.com.

buns+books

You probably would not expect in a discussion of librarianship for me to show a picture like Figure 2.8. How about:

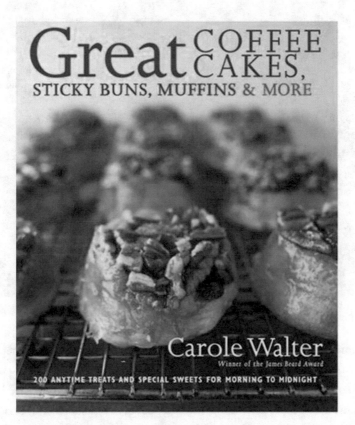

FIGURE 2.8: Buns+book.

woman+comfortable shoes

Would you expect Figure 2.9?

FIGURE 2.9: Woman+comfortable shoes. Image courtesy fotosearch.com.

While you might not expect them, once you do see the pictures, it is accepted. It is not confusing, just unexpected.

Why spend so much time on how people know, and its relational nature? Because it is at the heart of the questions that people ask and how reference service is successful. People construct these relationships through conversations. To provide an effective digital reference service, someone needs to successfully identify the existing relationships in a person with a question and build new relationships to fill an information need.

To take this out of the context of a game and make it a bit more real, take a look at this digital reference conversation from Oregon's L-Net service:[1]

librarian: hi Anonymous
anonymous: hi
librarian: so you are looking for a suggestion for a good new fantasy book? what do you like to read, to give me an idea where to start?

---

[1] http://www.oregonlibraries.net/archive/126733

anonymous: tithe, sunshine, twilight[2]

anonymous: that last one is twilight

librarian: ah, ok…so kind of the urban fantasy realm, maybe?

In this opening, we see an attempt to determine context. "Fantasy" is a pretty broad term (and very broad literary genre), so the librarian attempts to constrain the idea (later, we will talk about this as an agreement). The librarian does so by exchanging both examples, and a refined term "urban fantasy."

anonymous: by the way i am a tenager (if that helps)

librarian: is that Sunshine by Robin McKinley, or another one?

librarian: and yup that helps. :)

anonymous: yes!!

Once again the librarian constrains contexts to better target answers. Instead of the word game with words and pictures, the librarian is using book title and authors.

librarian: ok, I think I can help! let me look in my files…

anonymous: thanx

librarian: have you ever read any of Charles De Lint's books?

librarian: Like Blue Girl?

anonymous: no. never heard of it

librarian: ok, let me get you a plot description, plus some online booklists cause I bet there are some…hang on…

anonymous: k

librarian: ok, plot description from my catalog: New at her high school, Imogene enlists the help of her introverted friend Maxine and the ghost of a boy who haunts the school after receiving warnings through her dreams that soul-eaters are threatening her life.

librarian: are you a girl, by any chance? it's probably more fun for girls to read…

anonymous: yes. it sounds interesting

Here is an interesting point. In identifying *Blue Girl* as more appealing to a girl, the librarian is demonstrating two assumptions. The first is that pushing it, the librarian assumes anonymous is a girl (though the librarian does check after the fact). The librarian also assumes that *Blue Girl*, is in fact, better for girls. This is really a demonstration of the context the librarian has. One might argue that the librarian is now narrowing contexts without the user's consent.

---

[2] All transcripts are presented in their original form with misspelling and mistypes.

anonymous: thank you. bye.

librarian: wait, one more

anonymous: waiting

librarian: weblist, from Multnomah County:

librarian: http://www.multcolib.org/teens/ifyouliketwilight.html

librarian: are you out of time? there's so many books out there, but I guess those would help you with some ideas...

anonymous: my lunch is almost over. thanks again. bye

librarian: ah, ok. bye now! thanks for using LNet!

What happens when context and existing relationships are not taken into account? Quite simply, an inability to arrive at an answer. For example, I went online looking for a specific article from the New York Times on the mass of incorrect medical information available online for a proposal I was writing. In the actual digital reference conversation, the librarian started taking me to sites like the National Institutes for Health telling me that these resources had excellent information on health matters. The librarian completely missed the fact that I was looking for a specific article, and an article on bad information at that. In my mind, I had a relationship I was trying to complete:

> I Need<->Some article <->Bad medical information on the
> web<->Give me money to fix this problem

The librarian was trying to build a relationship like:

> User<->Has bad information<->Needs good information
> <->Here are good resources.

By not exploring these relationships, the librarian failed.

The story, by the way, has a positive ending that demonstrates the power of digital reference over traditional face-to-face reference. A supervising librarian read over the transcript, saw the real question and e-mailed me the proper citation (she even noted that the article I was looking for was really in the *Wall Street Journal*).

You can argue that this ability to understand relationships between known and unknown items is also the key to effective use of any digital library, and you would be right. We will come back to that idea soon enough; first, we better clarify what I mean by a conversation.

· · · ·

CHAPTER 3

Conversations

At the heart of any reference transaction is a conversation. It is a specialized type of conversation, between an expert and a user. Expert in this case is defined as someone along a sort of coordinate system with two axes: content expertise (knowledge of a given topic or area) and process expertise (knowledge of skills that are useful in a broad range of contexts). So a librarian, by and large, is a process expert. They have expertise in searching skills, for example. A volcanologist, when asked a question on volcanoes, answers as a content expert. Later, we will open up this reference process to more than just two individuals, but in any case, there is a conversation going on.

The definition of a conversation for this lecture is grounded in the conversation theory (Pask, 1976). This broad theory was developed by Gordon Pask in the 1960s and 1970s as part of his cybernetics work. Specifically, he wanted to teach machines to think. He thought the best place to start was with how people learned.

What he found was that people learn, or, in his word, know, through conversations. Conversations consist of four basic parts:

1. Conversants
2. Language
3. Agreements
4. Memory (represented in an entailment mesh).

Let us break these down and look at them in the context of digital reference.

3.1   CONVERSANTS

When we think of everyday conversations, we think of two or more people. It is not too far a stretch, then, for conversation theory to state that a conversation can be between two or more organizations as well. After all, an organization is just a group of people. This logic easily extends to two or more governments, or regions, or even societies. Possibly less intuitive is that the two or more parties in a conversation can be within the same person.

The idea of conversations between the individual and himself or herself is actually pretty well established. In education, there are discussions of metacognition and critical thinking where students are taught to reflect on activities (Bertland, 1986). In a much more common-sense approach, ask yourself, who are you talking to when you ask yourself questions ("does this shirt make me look fat," "should I go the long way and get bagels or just take the highway"). When you are reading, you are having an internal conversation. There is a chance that at some point in reading this lecture, you will ask yourself "what does he mean by that" or "does he *really* believe that?" You are engaging in a one-person conversation. Pask would say you are still, however, engaged in a conversation between multiple agents—these cognizing agents are just stored in a single skull.

3.2   LANGUAGE

So what are these two conversants, or agents, transmitting back and forth? Language. There is a lot of work in digital libraries, and information retrieval in particular, on the exchange of language. From early IR systems to natural language systems, digital libraries have struggled to take advantage of structures and regularity in language to find materials. One of the main advantages of virtual reference is that, by definition, it incorporates the most effective language processor on the face of the planet—a human being. That said, there is still plenty of room for two human beings to miscommunicate in a reference exchange. Much of this is due to the types of language being exchanged. In fact, the previous reference examples with fantasy literature and articles on health information demonstrate where language is used well and where miscommunication occurs.

Participatory librarianship, based on conversation theory, concerns itself with two levels of language being exchanged between conversants: L_0 and L_1. L_0 is the language exchanged between two conversants where at least one of the parties has little knowledge of the domain being discussed. It tends to be very directional (do this, now do this). Most of the discourse is negotiating meanings and terms at a very simple level. L_1, on the other hand, is exchanged between two parties with a high understanding of the domain discussed. Here, conversations tend to use special language and explore more "why" questions to establishing structural relationships between concepts.

Let us use a simple example to illustrate the difference in language levels. Let us take the following sentence:

Our catalog uses MARC to present our users with a great searching experience.

If you are a librarian, this is a meaningful sentence. You might even ask "how can MARC, as a bibliographic record format, impact a user's experience?" On the other hand, if you are not a librarian, this sentence is a jumble. Are we talking about catalogs, like from a store where I pick out

FIGURE 3.1: Search interface.

sweaters—who is Marc and why is he so helpful—do we really want to make it easy for drug users? As we saw in our previous word game, preexisting structures and contexts to words matter a lot. The more that relationships and contexts of words that are shared by conversants, the higher the level of discourse possible. High level of correlation equals L_1.

These levels of language have real implications for the systems we present to users. Systems can either attempt to work at differing levels of language, to bring users from L_0 to L_1, or bring the system from L_0 to L_1. Take the example of a search engine interface in Figure 3.1. This interface does little to educate the user about how to interact using high-level language. It is built around an assumption that users will be communicating their needs in L_0. The system will use complex algorithms and information retrieval techniques to make up for the fact it will probably be getting a very anemic query. If you do take the time to learn the language of this system, you can actually use some rather advanced language to improve your results (in this case, using a query language with +, -, ~, and quotes).

Reference and searching are often used in systems where there is an anticipated difference in the languages of the users and the system builders. In libraries, reference as a function came about because indexes and classification systems were too complex for many library users. The idea was to provide a human intermediary as a sort of bridge between a person with a question and the complex language used by library systems.

The second approach to designing systems is what Pask referred to as "learning systems" that endeavor to bring users from L_0 to L_1. This is actually one of the stated aims of traditional reference. As an intermediary is determining an answer to a question, s/he engages the user in the process and demonstrates the process. Let us take a look at another digital reference conversation from Oregon:

> **librarian**: Hi there! My name is Librarian and I am a librarian at Chemeketa Community College. Thanks for checking out the virtual reference service!
>
> **anonymous**: You're welcome
>
> **librarian**: We have another class of students visiting right now, and it is nice to see the interest…although a little busy.
>
> **librarian**: let's see what we can find for photos.
>
> **anonymous**: Thanks, we come back tomorrow if it gets too hectic
>
> **librarian**: that's okay…let me take a look. i'm going to pop out to the internet and do a little searching. Be right back.

Note that the librarian is not simply providing pictures and seeking feedback on the results, rather the librarian is guiding the user by example—showing the steps.

> **librarian**: Well—on the Statesman Journal site, we can search for photos.
>
> **librarian**: http://www.statesmanjournal.com/apps/pbcs.dll/article?AID=/20080608/ NEWS…
>
> **librarian**: Can you see this page? It has to do with class photos, but I am going to look for photos of your sports team. What is your team name?
>
> **anonymous**: Cavaliers
>
> **librarian**: The Cavaliers…any sport in particular?
>
> **anonymous**: Blanchet Catholic School Cavaliers
>
> **anonymous**: Volleyball was just in this weekm we'd like to see if there are others.. perhaps football or soccer
>
> **anonymous**: Should I go ahead and click on the link or will I loose you?
>
> **librarian**: i believe it will open in a new window…but here is a list of results for the Cavaliers, try clicking on one of these.

Note how the language begins to shift from simple direction (go here, fill in the blanks) to a slightly more complex discussion. Now they are not just talking about getting sports pictures, but specifying a sport and a team. The language used now assumes that there is a common understanding of sports. The user did not have to explain what volleyball was, for example.

librarian: http://salem.planetdiscover.com/sp?aff=1100&skin=100&keywords=
Blanchet+C...

anonymous: Thank you, I think we have enough for now. I'll let you go. Perhaps we can join you again.

librarian: please do! It is nice to hear from a class in Salem. Good luck with your research. ~Librarian

Other examples might be seen in help systems incorporated into many digital libraries that include tutorials and video demonstrations. However, the language shift in reference is different from other forms of refining results. Since Belkin and Oddy's (1980) Anomalous States of Knowledge work, the predominant approach in information retrieval has been the introduction of a feedback loop. Feedback and the rapid delivery of candidates that a user can accept or refute allow the user to get to a more precise retrieved answer. However, what we see in reference is an expansion of this idea. Here, the user and librarians actually educate each other and change language. The end result may be a more precise answer, but another is an expanded concept of the problem. In addition to the answer, the user (and librarian in this case) gained knowledge that can be used in additional information seeking.

One of the best examples of increasing language levels in systems can be seen in modern games. Where once games came with long and in-depth manuals, today complex games actually incorporate learning into the game itself. The first level is often a form of in-game tutorial familiarizing players with the basic mechanics of the game.

Of course, the approach of raising the user's language level is founded on the rather dubious assumption that a system can change the user. It is also antithetical to the user-centered paradigm dominant in today's system development world. A third approach is to assume the user is at L_1 and it is the system that needs to catch up. This may seem odd, as the user is the one asking the question, but remember, questions are sometimes used to refine knowledge, and the language exchanged between system and user is not always about questions. The use of tagging and annotation in web systems demonstrates this approach. Here, users incorporate their own language. Systems can then look for patterns in language use to provide information.

3.3   AGREEMENTS

So what is the goal of these conversants in exchanging language? Certainly just changing the language used is insufficient to gain knowledge. The ultimate goal of these exchanges is to reach agreements. In the word game, we used images and words to come to agreements on what a given word meant (for a given context). We then scaffold these agreements to explore more complex concepts. In the reference example on fantasy books, the librarian used titles and authors to reach agreement on the genre of book being looked for. In the reference conversation on sports images, there were a number of agreements that had to be reached before an answer was provided. The participants had to agree on what sport and what team was desired, for example.

In a face-to-face transaction, there are many methods of coming to and communicating agreements. A conversant may look for nodding or puzzled looks. In language exchange, there are often phrases such as "does that make sense" or "is that what you were looking for?" Small agreements then lead to larger understandings. This whole lecture is really a process of establishing and scaffolding agreements through language. Throughout the document, I am referencing concepts already (hopefully) established, and I am also foreshadowing new agreements yet to be made.

Agreements are made and simultaneously related to other agreements. It should be noted that this relating of agreements is a unique and internal process. That is to say that I may want to link a new concept to a very particular context in your mind but I cannot force that connection. You are ultimately responsible for your own connections. It should also be noted that two or more conversants can simply agree not to agree.

In virtual reference, coming to agreements must be established through some sort of negotiating process. Unlike face-to-face transactions, in virtual reference, there are few clues outside of text that can be used to create agreements. Some virtual reference tools supplement text exchange with features such as "page pushing," where experts can show users pages to come to some sort of agreement ("you mean something like this page"). In any case, in reference, the process of seeking agreements is central.

Let us go back to Oregon and look at another reference transaction:

librarian: Hi Anonymous,
anonymous: Hi librarian
librarian: I see your question about the book 'explain pain'
librarian: I think I can help you find it.
anonymous: yes, the author is David Butler and I cant seem to find it anywhere
They have just agreed on the general query. This general framework will now carry through the rest of the conversation.
librarian: so you looked in the library catalog and it wasn't there?
anonymous: That would be great. I looked in the Washington and Multnomah County DB and they didn't have it.
librarian: ok

They have agreed on previous steps in the information-seeking process. This will shape how the reference librarian looks for an answer. It also sets up an interesting power dynamic. What would happen if the reference librarian tried to look for the book at Washington and Multnomah? Would this anger the user, or embarrass the user if it was found? This seemingly simple agreement actually dominates the rest of the conversation (note the following pointers to interlibrary loan). It has been said that the most insulting question that can be asked in a digital reference service is "did you search Google?" There is an unstated agreement that the previous information seeking work of the user is to be respected and assumed to be valid. This is much more a social convention than good practice, however.

> **librarian**: just to verify, is this the book (from amazon)...
> **librarian**: http://www.amazon.com/Explain-Pain-David-Butler/dp/097509100X
> **anonymous**: Yes, this is the book

Now they have agreed on the actual object being sought.

> **anonymous**: as you can see, to purchase the book would be very expensive
> **librarian**: yes

They have agreed it is expensive. This is a seemingly simple agreement, but once again, it will dominate the rest of the transaction. The solution cannot be costly, and the librarian has just validated the decision of the user not to just buy the book. They are building rapport.

> **librarian**: it looks like some of the local colleges have it
> **librarian**: lets find the interlibrary loan service for tigard public library
> **anonymous**: how do we do that?
> **librarian**: I am just looking for the service on their web page
> **anonymous**: ah, ok

Note the language of agreement—"ok" and "yes."

> **librarian**: If we can't find it, I have a way to connect you with a Tigard Librarian over e-mail
> **librarian**: ok I found the link http://www.tigard-or.gov/library/using/borrowing.asp
> **librarian**: it sounds like they want you to make the request in-person—a lot of libraries have online forms

> **librarian**: scroll down to 'interlibrary loans'
> **anonymous**: ok, so i just email them at that email address?
> **librarian**: yes—and it says, "put ILL REQUEST as the "Subject" and also include your full name, library card number and home phone number in the request"

Agreement on the process of ILL.

> **anonymous**: Ok, I can manage that. Do you know of a specific library I can tell them has the book?
> **librarian**: they actually ahve more information than me
> **librarian**: but Mt. Hood Community College has it, for example
> **librarian**: usually, the ILL service likes to choose who they borrow from
> **anonymous**: Oh, ok.

Agree on how ILL works.

> **librarian**: they try to get it for free before they borrow for someone who charges
> **anonymous**: yeah, thats understandable.

More agreement on ILL. These little agreements are intended to put the user at ease—making him or her feel more in control of the process.

> **librarian**: and sometimes there are different editions
> **librarian**: but the fact that a few oregon colleges have it makes me think it shouldn't take too long
> **anonymous**: Well, thanks. I'll email them to there expectations and hopefully can get this book quickly.
> **anonymous**: Thanks again for your service!
> **librarian**: you're welcome
> **librarian**: is there antyhing more i can help you with today?
> **anonymous**: Nope, i'm good to go.

Agree that they are done.

> **librarian**: great—bye
> **anonymous**: bye

This example may make agreements seem trivial. Yet, they also make the agreements (or technically, my identification of agreements) evident even in seemingly straightforward transactions. If the librarian in the medical misinformation example had simply started by reaching agreement on the query, the whole transaction would not have failed.

It is also worth pointing to Marie Radford's work on question negotiation and encountering to see a much more refined analysis of the role of language and agreement types in reference.

3.4   MEMORY

Of course, to be useful, agreements must be stored so that they may be used later. This is our memory. What we also know from the word game and the discussions of agreements and language is that these agreements are stored in relationships to one another. The expression of these agreements and their relationships in a given domain is known as an entailment mesh.

It would be akin to beating a dead horse to talk about contexts and relationships at this point. Instead, let us consider how these relationships and externalized memory are organized and stored. This disconnection between how we learn and how libraries, digital or otherwise, organize materials is at once the greatest reason for reference and reference's greatest challenge.

James Burke, a journalist and historian, creates thematic journeys through history, focusing on how technological achievements from the past impact our current world. In one such journey, he talks about how the first crusades to "liberate" Islamic Spain led to modern universities. In short, when the crusaders took Toledo in Southern Spain, they discovered great libraries. One such library contained over 440,000 volumes—more than were present in the entirety of France at the time. What followed was an unprecedented flood of translated Greek and long lost treatises in science, philosophy, and law. Young nobles in Italy, seeking to get ahead, hired tutors and translators to teach them the newly rediscovered knowledge. Eventually, the students pooled their resources, building communal living and learning spaces and hiring teams of tutors. These facilities became the first colleges. The practice of students hiring faculties lasted well into the 19th century, and much of the concepts of faculties and discipline-specific colleges shape modern universities to this day.

This trip through history is full of differing relationships. To truly understand it (and agree with it) requires knowledge of Islamic Spain, Renaissance Italy, and universities. The story can also be extended, taking into account historian John M. Barry's history of modern medical education in the United States. Barry talks about how modern medical education began at Johns Hopkins University, including reforming the inherent conflict of interest in students directly paying the salaries of their professors and an increased focus on experimental research. Table 3.1 lays out how this one historical thread crosses over traditional classification schemes (in this case, Library of Congress Classifications):

TABLE 3.1: History of modern medical education in the United States	
BURKE'S HISTORY	**LIBRARY OF CONGRESS**
Islamic Spain	DP97.3-160.8 Moorish domination and the Reconquest
Libraries of Moorish Spain	Z4-8 History of books and bookmaking
Renaissance Italy	DG532-537.8 Renaissance
Early universities	LA173-186 Higher education
Modern universities	LB2326.4-2330 Institutions of higher education
Medical education	LC1051-1072 Professional education
Johns Hopkins	LD13-7251 Universities and colleges

What we see in this chart is that, in attempting to make knowledge portable and easily accessible, it is often torn from its original contexts and aligned to some taxonomy (classification). This taxonomy is itself the result of an ongoing conversation (around the question "how do we organize the world"). As systems get more functional, they should be able to allow users to make use of their own relationships and not map to some common language scheme.

3.4.1   Knowledgebase Problem

Let us, at this point, take some time to discuss digital reference knowledgebases, as they are the most concrete representation of memory in digital reference. Almost at the inception of answering questions online came the concept of storing these questions and answers (for discussions of knowledgebases in digital reference, see Bry, 2000; Pomerantz & Silverstein, 2003). While there was not necessarily a specific reason or application at first, several have emerged:

Answer Reuse. One of the early influences of digital reference was the help desk industry. On its surface, this makes sense. After all, questions are asked and answered with some technology mediating the process. One of the basic premises in help desks is the concept of saturation. Saturation is that point when all incoming questions have been asked before. Once saturation is hit, you can quickly identify the question type and automatically send out a preexisting answer. It was assumed that reference questions are the same—they are not. Help desks are targeted to a specific product or process. They are bounded, and therefore, the world of possible questions and answers is finite. I call it the "broken toaster syndrome." When you call up a help desk about a broken toaster, the agent on the other end of the call walks you through a script (really a decision tree) of possible problems ("did you put a fork in it?" "is it plugged in?"). If the problem is not in the domain of known answers, it is actually bumped out of the system ("I'm going to have to transfer you to a product specialist."). Increasingly, the human being is being taken out of these decision trees, and users are expected to navigate a phone tree or go online to browse the "knowledgebase."

While some digital library reference fits into this category of question answering, most do not. In contrast to saturation, libraries (digital and otherwise) view each question as unique. Even if the basic concepts are the same, there is often a contextual twist that will make the question unique. Libraries focus (or should focus) on context. The domain of possible answers becomes infinite. While patterns might emerge, human intermediaries provide context and conversation, not simply navigational support through a finite set of answers. This explains why help desk packages have generally been failures in reference contexts. It also explains why, in the age of the Internet reference, experts find that a good number of their answers refer to resources well beyond the bounds of a single collection.

Frequently Asked Questions (FAQ) Generation. While every question may be unique, there are certainly patterns in the questions being asked. For example, after the 9/11 attacks, AskERIC, a digital reference service of the U.S. Department of Education, received a spike in their questions. These questions were not about the attacks but, rather, on Islam. The service quickly developed resources on Islam. It did not mean there would not be new questions on the topic, or that these resources answered all the possible questions, it was simply a trend that, at a high-level of abstraction, answered general questions. FAQs in a bound context are seen as time savers. In open domains, they often generate new questions. In some services, FAQs are derived through some sort of process (such as classifying answers). In other services, they are much more a reaction of reference staff to their own work.

Collection Building. If trends in questions can be determined, and resources such as FAQs can be developed, the next logical step is reference authoring. Reference authoring is the process of using reference transactions to create resources and collections. It is a transformation process that starts with raw transcripts, leads to some intermediary step (like identification of more general classes of transcripts), and some final product. While one of these products might be a FAQ, there are much more interesting ones. It might be a searchable repository of questions and answers. The Ask Dr. Math service actually wrote mathematics textbooks from their transactions. AskERIC sought to build its entire digital library collection from the questions asked, a process Pomerantz (2003) referred to as "an accretion model."

One project, Reference Extract, takes yet another approach. URLs are extracted from virtual reference transcripts. For each URL, a frequency count is calculated (how many times did reference experts point to this URL?). The URLs themselves are used as seeds to a web search engine. The frequency counts are used to rank the results of searches, much as Google ranks results by the number of incoming links a given page has.

Administrative Control. The preceding purposes of digital reference knowledgebases are oft discussed, but there are few examples beyond FAQs of successful implementations. This has led many reference experts to question the overall value of a knowledgebase to begin with. This overlooks the near universal use of knowledgebases to derive usage statistics and provide quality control. Many virtual reference services have relatively detailed statistics of not simply how many questions have been received, but from whom, and in what environment. Further, many services use knowledgebases to provide quality control. Therefore, archived transcripts are examined for good and bad practice, or to provide second tier review. It is also worth noting that much of the evaluation and research work in digital reference is based on a knowledgebase of existing questions and answers (see Ward, 2003; Mon and Janes, 2002; Radford and Connaway, 2007).

Perhaps the broadest approaches to knowledgebases can be characterized as deductive versus inductive approaches. In deductive approaches, questions, answers, and/or transcripts are slotted into a preexisting classification scheme. Some of this slotting is done by the reference staff, and some is done by the users (possibly edited by some administrator). There are some very real drawbacks to such approaches:

- Context dependencies: Information in knowledgebases is very context-dependent. It is quite possible that the only application of the information in a digital reference transcript is to that given interchange between librarian and patron.
- Metadata creation: Time, labor, and money are involved in creating metadata for transcripts and digital reference interchanges so that they may be later discovered and retrieved by end users. While some of this effort may be part of the reference process itself (for example, classifying a question for distribution in QuestionPoint), it may still require effort to confirm and refine this classification data for inclusion in a knowledgebase.
- Chunking: It is well known that users will ask several questions in both real-time and asynchronous transactions. How those questions and answers are "broken apart" is often dependent on human intervention and a great deal of interpretation.

- Fact shifting and temporal dependencies: Answers to reference questions are often time-dependent. From the name of the U.S. president to the height of Mount Everest, answers to even simple questions change. These changes, while concrete, are often hard to track over time. This does not even take into account "gray" areas, where an answer or fact to apply to a question is a matter of choice among equally good options.

These are not minor limitations to overcome. Many have looked at these problems and concluded that reference knowledgebases are useless beyond basic administrative functions. At the very least, the maintenance of a deductive system will be labor-intensive.

Others have looked at the limitations of the deductive approach and tried a different, inductive approach. This approach is characterized as deriving structure or utility from the reference data itself. At a very simple level, this would be making the reference data searchable. Certainly, the Reference Extract and Dr. Math examples from above are inductive approaches. There has also been a discussion of more advanced inductive approaches utilizing data mining techniques (Nicholson & Lankes, 2007). In the end, inductive approaches seem to be a more fruitful approach.

3.5 LOOKING AT THE REFERENCE TRANSACTION AS A CONVERSATION

In the reference interview, or the reference encounter as Marie Radford calls it, the expert and user engage in an active conversation to come to an understanding of an information need (for more on the reference interview and reference encountering, take a look at the works of Radford, 2001; Abels, 1996; Nilsen, 2005). Once the boundaries of this need are determined, the expert can apply their expertise to fulfill the need. This is often an interactive process with a great deal of back and forth. Of course, there are plenty of examples where experts do not engage in this negotiation and simply use their own contexts to fill in for an interview. From conversation theory, we can assume that this strategy, using an intermediary's context over a user-supplied one, will work when the possible contexts of a query are low (but still commonly held) or very common. Known item search, for example, presents a system with a very low number of possible contexts—how many authors have the name "R. D. Lankes," for example. Likewise, a question about the presidential debates during an election year in the United States will most likely be about the current election and the most recent debate.

However, the context of the query, which we will define as how the answer can fit into a user's set of preexisting agreements, is often unique to the person asking the question, or the context of the question is ambiguous. In this case, reference work without an interview is simply not effective. Take two examples from virtual reference studies. The first, by Sylvia Southwick (2001), looked at digital reference transactions in a medical setting. Here, reference librarians had full knowledge of the people asking questions and would answer the questions based on the librarian's context (more precisely, the context the librarian assumed the person asking the question had). Therefore, a question asked by a nurse was always answered with printed resources because the librarians "knew" that nurses were not too technically proficient. This led to a standing puzzle on the part of the nurses as to why they always got paper, when they would have preferred electronic documents.

The second example is derived from Makiko Miwa's (2000) study on virtual reference and information problem solving. Miwa wanted to know if where a user was in an information problem solving process would affect the questions they asked. What she found was that the text of a question remained very consistent but the context of the question changed radically. So, take a Ph.D. student—we will call her Joanne—asking a question about her dissertation topic. At the beginning of the dissertation process, she might ask a question like "can you tell me all the articles that deal with topic X." Joanne is looking for a pool of studies she can use to explore. To a degree, the completeness of the produced list of citations is not as important as their variety and number. The day before she submits the dissertation Joanne may once again ask "can you tell me all the articles that deal with topic X." Here, she is looking for a complete list to see if she missed any articles; the same question with radically different contexts.

This reality of reference as a conversation has long existed. There have been many practices that have grown out of an implicit assumption of reference. The next chapters shall explore how the implicit understanding of reference as conversation has shaped digital reference. Later chapters will reengage the participatory concepts to look at how digital reference may evolve in the future.

· · · ·

CHAPTER 4

Digital Reference in Practice

To this point, we have been looking at the reference function of a digital library at a conceptual level. However, as with many digital library applications, much of this conceptual work came after an active period of implementation, experimentation, and praxis. This practice-driven experimentation continues to this day, and there is a rich and real dialog between practitioners and researchers. In this chapter, I would like to cover key aspects of digital reference that have emerged from practice activities. The broadest model of virtual reference practice available is the general digital reference model (Pomerantz et al., 2004), seen in Figure 4.1.

The model starts with a question from a *user* entered through a *question acquisition* process. This might be an e-mail, web form, or simply an instant message request. *Triage* is a process where the appropriate answer source is indentified. The process might be manual, with some administrator determining how to handle the question, or it may be completely automated. Examples of automated processes include simply assigning the question to the next available reference expert or sending the user a canned response that matches some keywords in the question. After (or in some cases if) the question reaches an *expert*, he or she engages in *answer formulation*—some process to find or create an answer. That answer is forwarded off to the original user, and entered, in some form, into a *Q&A archive*, or knowledgebase. Then, as discussed in the previous section on knowledgebases, some form of *tracking* and *resource creation* can take place. Let us explore the stages of this model in a bit more depth, highlighting common practice and significant milestones in each. Since we have spent a good amount of time on questions, let us start with *question acquisition*.

4.1 QUESTION ACQUISITION

Question acquisition refers to transferring an initial user question to a digital reference service. It is not a negotiated question (that will come in answer formulation). It can be as simple as an e-mail message. In so-called chat reference services, which offer real-time interactions with reference experts, it is the initial form that a user fills out to get connected to an expert.

So what is there to talk about in terms of getting a question from the user into a digital reference process? A lot. This stage of the model represents the primary interface to the user. As such, work in human–computer interaction and usability is relevant. However, this is not a lecture about

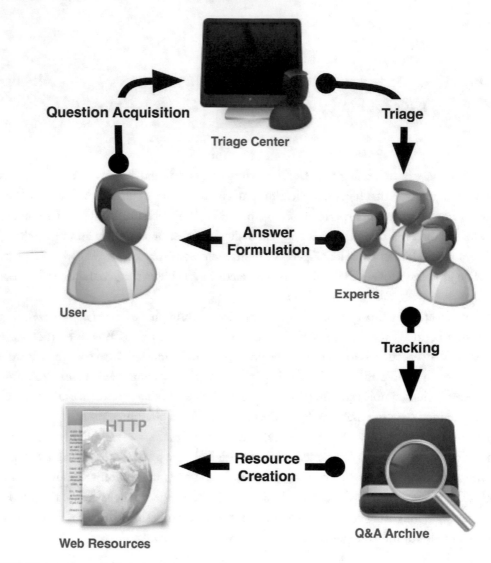

FIGURE 4.1: General digital reference model.

these things, so I will focus on two aspects of digital reference practice as it relates to getting questions: preinterviews and service placement.

Preinterview simply refers to the kind of information users have to provide and understand before their question is actually processed. In the early days of digital reference, many services simply provided a form that asked users for their question and their e-mail addresses. This form often also contained some service expectation information ("we will answer your question in two days," or "understand your question may be made public"). For digital reference services with plenty of experts to handle their volume of questions (and this includes a majority of traditional library organizations), this was, and still is, sufficient (though they may also ask for some additional "membership" information like a zip code or library card number). However, for high-volume services, this form was refined to speed up the process.

For example, for services that operated primarily via e-mail or asynchronously, going back to a user for additional detail on their questions is time consuming. To speed up the process, these services instituted more elaborate forms in lieu of an interactive "reference interview." Users were asked not only for their question, but to self-identify what type of user they were (often around age or education level), what resources they had already checked, and the ultimate use of their answer (thus violating the traditional library practice of never asking someone why they needed to know something—the users did not seem to mind the question).

Several services experimented with a "sandwich interface" found commonly on self-help systems (see Bry, 2000). Here, a user would enter a question and the system would scrape the question for keywords, conduct a search for existing answers, and present the user with preexisting information. The user could still forward their question to an expert if the automated process did not work. Initially, this dramatically cut down the number of incoming questions. The problem came when several services looked at the resources users chose as their answers, and found about 90% of the time, they did not actually seem to answer the question asked. This approach also harkens back to our discussion of saturation and assumptions about repeat questions.

Another interesting finding from practice relates to privacy. While one of the core principles of libraries is that reference interviews must be private, there are plenty examples of digital reference services that actually create public archives of their reference work. Almost all of these services give the user a choice to either keep their transactions private or public. The overwhelming choice of users is public. This is not meant to dismiss the issue of privacy. There are still many who feel one-to-one private conversations are essential for reference.[1] However, it does call for a serious understanding of patrons and their understandings and needs for privacy. My opinion is that librarians feel privacy is so important that they do not even give users a chance to decide on the issue. By removing this choice, it is a lost opportunity to work with and educate users about the real importance of the topic.

4.2   TRIAGE

Many of the early digital reference services were high-volume AskA services (such as Ask A Scientist, Ask A Volcanologist, etc.) that took questions in via the web and/or e-mail. Almost all of these

---

[1] http://www.oregonlibraries.net/staff/2008/05/09/dave_lankes_oregon_virtual_reference_summit_2008

services took days to produce answers. Almost all of these services instituted some sort of manual triage process. This process created a buffer between incoming questions and experts. A question was screened for spam, to determine if it was a repeat, or even if it was answerable (no e-mail address meant no way to get an answer back to the user). Experts were seen as expensive and valuable assets, and their time should be maximized. Even when services pooled experts, triage processes refined and edited questions (meaning the production of knowledgebases and Q&A archives at the end of the process were greatly facilitated).

Here is an interesting divergence between library-based digital reference and other digital reference services. In most library-based digital reference today (excluding help desks), there are ample experts to answer questions, so triage is automated. Here, questions are put into a "next avail-able" queue. This is also based on the assumption that all librarians are equally qualified to answer all questions. The consequence has been that, in library-based digital reference, triage development has virtually halted.

In higher capacity services that utilize much more specialized and scarce topical expertise, and in the help desk world, triage still remains a central point of investigation. There was some work conducted as part of the National Science Foundation's National Science Digital Library that pointed to some promising areas of development. Work by Bruce Kroft's group at the University of Massachusetts Amherst in conjunction with the author and the Wondir Corporation sought to develop automatic triage mechanisms that could direct a question to an automated answer source (like a search engine) or to a human expert. Much promise was found in automatically identifying a questions level of ambiguity (the higher the ambiguity of the question, the more need for clarifi-cation and a human intermediary). Jeffry Pomerantz also did some excellent work into automatic classification of questions—believing that the type of question asked should indicate the type of resource needed to provide an answer.

Frankly, it is a shame that the development of triage has either stalled or happens behind the closed doors of help desk companies. Certainly a robust and generalizable utility (or algorithms, or rules) that could help anticipate the resources needed to provide an answer would revolutionize reference. Alas, it may be an impossible dream. Just look at the periodic start and stop of for-fee digital reference services. Since the early days of the web, companies with names like Mining Co., Google Answers, Wondir, ChaCha, and more have seen a potential bonanza in charging users to provide answers. All have either failed, changed models, or become virtual wastelands of semian-swered questions and personal soapboxes. I even used to write and talk about a "question economy" that would create a virtual cloud of expertise where questions and answers could be bid, bought, and sold like a sort of stock market.

It is a sexy idea that turns out to be a trap. The trap is to assume that a question is in some way directly related to the process needed to develop an answer. In other words, that you can anticipate the resources needed to get an answer from just the question. For example, if I asked you "what is the boiling point of ethanol," do you think that question is easy to answer or hard? You might think it would be easy. It is a factual answer, very specific, with little room for ambiguity. This is certainly what the Times' Educational Supplement (http://www.timeshighereducation.co.uk/story.asp?sectioncode=26&storycode=401533&c=1) thought when they called up a score of academic libraries in the UK and reported that "Only two of 20 libraries were able to provide the correct boiling point of ethanol, making it the most incorrectly answered question in the 2008 survey." The Times implied that the wrong answers were a result of librarians using Wikipedia, which had the wrong answer. It turns out the librarians and Wikipedia were not the only ones who were wrong. The boiling point is listed at four different temperatures in a sample of 10 different standard reference books consulted for the study.

How about another example? What is your social security number? There is a pretty easy question to answer—for you. We all hope it is a hard question to answer for anyone else. There will always be questions that are easy to answer for you, but hard for me. There are, as Monty Python brilliantly pointed out in the Holy Grail's discussion of the average migratory speed of swallows, unanticipated complexities in a question that only become apparent in the process of developing an answer.

So if you cannot fully anticipate the effort necessary to answer a question before you actually answer it, how can you value the transaction before it is complete? More to the point, who is willing to commit to a price without confidence in the estimate?

4.3   ANSWER FORMULATION

Still, questions do get answered. In digital reference, they get answered with the aid of an "expert"; as discussed earlier, expertise is defined along the two axes of content expertise and process expertise. Looking through the volume of publications in digital reference, a large proportion of them are taken up with the problems of answer formulation. This is not really surprising since the answer is the point of the whole service.

Discussions of answer formulation range from process ("look in these resources, then these"), to policies ("we only answer from open web resources"), to structure ("first repeat the question, then bibliographic resources, then . . ."). Perhaps the most significant discussions center on the question of quality. In other words, what constitutes a good answer?

While we are now deep into the practicalities of virtual reference, it is worth noting that the terms "good," "quality," and "answer" are very much part of an ongoing debate in the reference world. Part of the purpose of presenting the conversation theory is to sidestep these philosophical debates. An answer is an agreement (or series of agreements). It is also the best that can be hoped for. Without an agreement, no amount of data transferred between expert and user will actually inform anyone. In this light, the ongoing debate about quality can be seen as a field-wide conversation to seek agreement of "good" and "bad" answers from a service perspective. Therefore, they are important conversations, but do not be fooled into thinking they are the aspiration of the users—just the aspiration of the services themselves.

The debate of what constitutes a good answer is as old as reference itself. I should point out that this is very much a library-generated conversation. Help Desks and Topical AskA services tend to have domain-specified definitions of quality answers. Libraries, on the other hand, have always dealt with an enormous gamut of interpretive situations (Saxton and Richardson, 2002). The result was an attitude that dominated reference for nearly a century (and still impacts reference education)—the central concept of bias. Reference answers should be unbiased. If there are multiple views on a subject, all views should be presented. Librarians in the days of the physical-only library were even taught to bring users to the appropriate shelf (maybe book) but not to bring up a specific page as it might influence the user.

Hernon and McClure (1987) stirred things up with their study of reference and the resulting 55% rule. Their data showed that, when there was a known answer to a factual question, librarians only gave the correct answer 55% of the time. As you can imagine from reading this lecture, the definition of "factual" has been debated ever since. At least once every 5 years, someone takes aim at the nuances of the 55% rule and why it is too low (see Durrance, 1989; Saxton and Richardson, 2002).

A sort of midpoint between defining "right" answers, where there must be a definitive right and wrong answer, and a stance that any answer could be right given the right context has emerged with the development of quality standards. These standards seek to define a range of practices and beliefs that can be agreed upon. A group of libraries and researchers came together around the question of quality standards for virtual reference. The end result was a series of quality standards (McClure et al., 2002) for virtual reference services:

- Courtesy: The behavior of the library's or institution's staff
- Accuracy: The "correctness" of answers provided by digital reference staff
- Satisfaction: Users' determination of their success in interacting with the digital reference service
- Repeat users: The percentage of users that reuse a service after first encounters
- Awareness: The population user group's knowledge that the service exists
- Cost: The cost per digital reference

These high-level standards were derived from a more concrete set of performance measures:

- Descriptive statistics and measures: Statistics and measures to determine the scale and scope of a digital reference service.

TABLE 4.1: Performance measures				
DESCRIPTIVE	**LOG**	**USER**	**COST**	**STAFF**
Number of digital reference questions received	Number of digital reference sessions	Awareness of service	Cost of digital reference service	Percent of staff time spent overseeing technology
Number of digital reference responses	Usage of digital reference service by day of the week	Accessibility of service	Cost of digital reference service as a percent of total reference budget	Percent of staff time spent assisting users with technology
Number of digital reference answers	Usage of digital reference service by time of day	Expectations for service	Cost of digital reference service as a percent of total library or organizational budget	
Total reference activity	User's browser	Other sources user tried		
Percentage of digital reference questions to total reference questions	User's platform	Reasons for use		
Digital reference correct answer fill rate		Reasons for non use		
Digital reference completion rate		Satisfaction with staff		

		TABLE 4.1: (*Continued*)		
DESCRIPTIVE	**LOG**	**USER**	**COST**	**STAFF**
Number of unanswered digital reference questions		Delivery mode satisfaction		
Type of digital reference questions received		Impact of service on user		
Total number of referrals		Additional services that need to be offered		
Saturation rate		User demographic data		
Sources used per question				
Repeat users (return rate)				

- Log analysis: Statistics that can be derived from analysis of logs generated by web and digital reference software packages
- User satisfaction measures: Statistics and metrics seeking to understand the user view of a digital reference service.
- Cost: Measures that gage outlay of financial resources to run an ongoing digital reference effort.
- Staff time expended: Measures to determine staff time dedicated to digital reference

Finally, these measures were broken into a series of metrics; their names (not accompanying equations) are listed in Table 4.1.

There are a few things you should know about these standards. The first is that they apply beyond the answers produced by the service. The other is that—and as one of the creators of these measures, I can say this—they make a fundamental assumption that ultimately limits their utility. They assume that all aspects of a digital reference service can be evaluated in relation to the questions received. That is, these measures, like so many before them, take all the activities of a digital reference service and divide them by the number of questions received (particularly in terms of cost).

There are also few explicit metrics for capturing the development of resources (like FAQs) that answer user questions before they are ever formally asked. Yet, as the previous discussion on knowledgebases points out, there is a rich area for exploration in the next parts of the general digital reference model, tracking and resource creation.

4.4 TRACKING AND RESOURCE CREATION

Digital reference is different from traditional face-to-face or even telephone models. Why? In face-to-face reference settings, it is very hard to create a record of the transaction. This is the reason that classical library reference statistics tend to be anemic (to say the least). In digital reference, however, it is the exact opposite case. Reference questions sit in e-mail inboxes, instant messaging logs (on the user's, expert's, and often IM provider's machines), service transcript, and web logs. In this way, digital reference becomes a durable authoring process that creates a "trackable" record.

Tracking in the model refers to a process of identifying trends in the questions received by a digital reference service and the answers that service produces. It can be as simple as a sense of patterns identified by experts, to a complex quantitative report on question topics and referenced resources (say, using the metrics from the quality standards work above). A digital reference service tracks its functions (a sort of formative evaluation) to improve service.

For example, as described earlier, immediately after the terrorist attacks of 9/11, AskERIC, a virtual reference service that answered questions in the education field, saw a significant increase in questions it received. Tracking processes showed that the bulk of these new questions were not about terrorism, or the 9/11 event, but on Islam. By identifying this trend, AskERIC could quickly assemble guides and pathfinders on the topic and fulfill a clear need in their user community.

Tracking, when done well, improves service. This extends beyond question/answering into all aspects of a digital library. By offering question/answering services, digital libraries gain authentic data in an unobtrusive way on the operations of the whole library operation. If a question is repeated often, it may indicate that there is either a gap in the collection (if the resource does not exist) or a design and/or navigation issue (if the resource is there but is not being found). AskERIC provides another example in this respect.

The AskERIC service was funded by the U.S. Department of Education. The service received a set amount of money per question, creating an incentive to respond to more questions.

However, the service had a cap on the money it could receive, creating a more refined incentive to keep questions at a given level. Too high, and resources (and incentive) to answer questions ran out; too low, and the service had a hard time sustaining staffing. In one lull in questions, the staff sought to increase questions. They added a banner that said "got a question? AskERIC" to the homepage of the service. Even though the "ask a question" button was also on the homepage (but much smaller), the banner led to a jump in questions. Through tracking and experimentation, it was found that use of the banner led to a predictable jump in questions. Further refined tracking lead to a system of banner placement (where to display it on the site, and for how long) that guaranteed that the number of questions always hit the "sweet spot" near the maximum number of questions.

4.4.1   Resource Creation

One of the differences between digital reference in a library context and digital reference as it has been implemented in digital library environments is that of resource creation. I have already talked about one type of resource creation common across digital reference environments: the knowledge-base. I have also mentioned some other examples of resource creation from textbooks to FAQs. However, in traditional library environments, digital reference is used to create isolated reference collections, while in digital libraries, they are seen as part of a much more central building activity. For example, with Expert Voices, a system built as part of the National Science Digital Library, answers were used to build a collection of previous answers, and also used as annotations to existing resources held in the digital library collection. In a study of top AskA services (Lankes, 1998), all of the services tied answering questions into building stand-alone web resources that had a life outside of the Q&A process.

One question this approach leads to is of coherence. That is, if you build a collection based on questions, do you build a coherent collection, where all the questions and answers relate to some central topic or collection focus, or do you add resources at the periphery of a focus, where the existing resources negate the need to ask questions on a topic, and only leave "out of scope" questions from users? One way to answer this is to look at the resources cited by services. The reasoning goes like this: as part of answering a question, a service references resources (in this case, web resources); to the extent that these answers represent the questions asked, the resources they cite will also be representative of the questions. By looking at the distribution of these citations, one should be able to glean how coherent the questions and answers are. Or, if that is too convoluted: if experts are citing the same stuff over and over again, the questions being asked must cluster. So citation analysis is one way to determine whether building a collection based on Q&A will be coherent or not.

Take a look at the graph in Figure 4.2 of the references cited by the AskERIC virtual reference service over 3 years. Each color band represents a different URL. Note the broad orange and

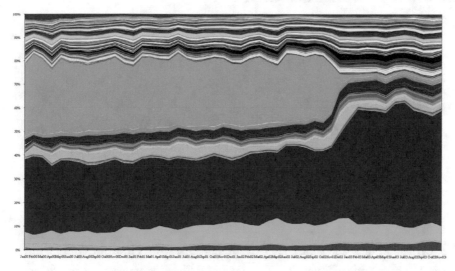

FIGURE 4.2: AskERIC citation pattern.

dark blue bands. The orange band is orders.edrs.com, and the dark blue is www.edrs.com. Since AskERIC was answering questions on the process of education, and included citations from the ERIC Database, it makes sense that it frequently cited how to order paper copies of these documents. Note how, three fourths of the way through the graph, the orange band disappears while the dark blue one expands. This was when the ERIC Document and Reproduction Service changed their web site and dropped a separate web site just for ordering. What this charts shows is an amazing level of coherence in a service's citation pattern.

Now, take a look at the citation pattern for AskNSDL, the service that evolved into Expert Voices discussed above, over 17 months in Figure 4.3. Note the visual randomness in the graph. There is very little consistency from month to month. It would be difficult to say that there is some coherent scope to the questions or resources. One might conclude this is from the differences in the mission of the two virtual reference services. Whereas AskERIC answers questions about education, AskNSDL answers questions from any area of science. Of course, this assumes that the field of education is relatively narrow. This is a very hard argument to make. Instead, the data seem to point to the preparation of the experts providing the answers.

AskERIC queries were answered by librarians and library science students. AskNSDL answers came from scientists with deep training in their given disciplines. Librarians are taught to cite, and even instructed in criteria of good and bad web sites. The truth is that the NSDL scientists do not cite that much in their answers because they are answering from their own knowledge. If you

FIGURE 4.3: AskNSDL citation pattern.

want further evidence, take a look at 3 months of citations from QuestionPoint, a virtual reference cooperative across hundreds of libraries. The topics and libraries are very diverse (academic libraries answering questions from scholars, to rural public libraries answering the questions of school chil-

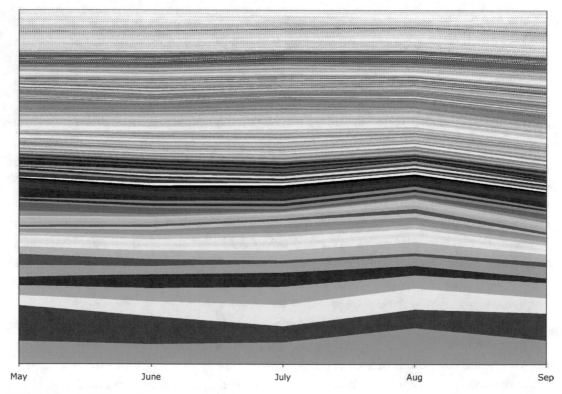

FIGURE 4.4: QuestionPoint citation pattern.

dren, to government librarians answering the questions of congressmen). With all this diversity, one would expect a very chaotic pattern. However, look at Figure 4.4. This is even more consistent than AskERIC. While there are a lot of bands (different sites), they are cited consistently.

Therefore, will the output of virtual reference services end up in a nice coherent collection, or a scatter shot of unrelated answers? Of course, the answer is that it depends. However, it does appear that the preparation of the experts is the key to the answer.

4.5   DURABILITY OF THE GENERAL DIGITAL REFERENCE MODEL

I can already hear it now—what about real-time, instant messaging or chat reference? This model looks a lot like an asynchronous model. If you are not saying that, you were not doing digital reference at the turn of this century. There was a great deal of debate around the question of synchronous versus asynchronous digital reference. Is it not fundamentally different to be conversing in real time with a patron versus going back and forth over e-mail? The answer appears to be no. I have argued that the only real difference is "lag time" (the idea was actually first put forth by Bruce Croft during the Digital Reference Research Symposium). All the steps are there, they just happen at different intervals. While I would love to say that I settled the question, truth be told, most people do not ask this question anymore because in libraries, at least, real-time interactions have become the predominant mode.

However, and I hate to do this to my own model, I think the lifespan of the general digital reference model is coming to an end; not that it is invalid, or that it does not pertain to the bulk of digital reference as currently conducted. Rather, the model is based on an ingrained and unstated assumption in the conduct of reference. That is that reference is a one-to-one activity. In the future (and increasingly in the present), the idea that the expert and user sit on different sides of a system wall or process is coming to an end, which, of course, leads us to talk about the future.

· · · ·

CHAPTER 5

Digital Reference and a New Future

The irony of talking about the future of digital reference is that, of course, digital reference was supposed to be the future. Answering questions online, chat environments, page pushing, video interactions, and reference via mobile phones are all examples of discussions in how digital reference is conducted. In a real way, digital reference has always been about the future and a field seeking new approaches. Where most library services have grown into hierarchical consortia, reference has turned into a series of peer-to-peer exchanges. Where much of the information world has been driven to standardization, reference has more often than not developed standards of all sorts and then promptly ignored them. However, one part of reference has steadfastly refused to yield to reinvention—the primacy of the one-to-one interaction.

In face-to-face reference, we have a librarian sitting at a desk waiting for questions. Therefore, the user comes into the library's space, has to leave their current work environment (the computer they were on, their office, their desk, etc.), approaches a desk built around the needs of a librarian, and explains his/her problem to a person they barely know. Is it any wonder that patrons assume that the librarians are experts in the content of their question, not just the process? Aside from potentially scaring off patrons, this system puts librarians in an awkward position. Librarians have to look approachable and convince patrons that, one, they are not bothered by answering questions, and, two, not knowing a content area is still useful.

One might counter that digital reference has solved many of these problems. However, we still invite users to come to our web sites and engage in our tools (of which the expert's tool set is much more powerful and ultimately controls the whole interaction). Therefore, while reference is a conversation, it is hardly a conversation where the user can do much more than follow the rules we establish.

Perhaps the largest constraint placed on the reference conversation is the fact that it is modeled (in person and online) as a one-to-one interaction. Even in settings of digital reference cooperatives that use referral systems, the underlying process is seen as one librarian and one patron. This is odd, as, time after time, when we seek to define digital reference, we do not include this aspect. Remember those definitions of virtual reference from the beginning of the lecture? OCLC defined digital reference as "Using computer and communications technology to provide reference service to patrons anytime and anywhere." The Digital Reference Research Agenda defined it as "the use of human intermediation to answer questions in a digital environment." This notion of one-to-one conversation was even missing from the RUSA's definition:

> Virtual reference is reference service initiated electronically, often in real-time, where patrons employ computers or other Internet technology to communicate with reference staff, without being physically present. Communication channels used frequently in virtual reference include chat, videoconferencing, Voice over IP, co-browsing, e-mail, and instant messaging.

Is there something about answering questions online that necessitates one librarian and one patron? While we can make an argument that certain situations require one-on-one work, say, to preserve privacy, to prevent the ambiguity of multiple answers, or perhaps to build an ongoing user relationship, in many cases, it is the result of tradition and existing practice based on limited resources in a physical world. Getting input on questions was expensive.

What if, however, we increase the pool of expertise available to answer questions? What if barriers such as queuing in lines or holding on the telephone were removed? Certainly, then, reference could be a more social experience. There are, of course, plenty of examples of a more group-based question answering. On the Internet alone, there are mailing lists, web forums, and the like. Yet, we can ask, are these examples of virtual reference? They meet the definitions. In fact, the only reason we might exclude them is because they are not formally seen as an activity of reference staff at institutions called libraries.

Is there something special about librarians that create the phenomenon "digital reference" other than a term of practice? Perhaps. Certainly, libraries approach reference from a very different perspective than most Internet users on mailing lists. Librarians are (or should be) trained not only in resources, but the very process of question answering and negotiation (or, as Radford has called it, encountering). After all, anyone can nail together two boards, but that does not make one a carpenter. Librarians bring to question answering a suite of principles and ethics. Also, as part of a larger institutional focus on information organization, there is at least the opportunity for the information exchanged in a reference transaction to be linked to many other information dissemination activities (including collection development, the writing of pathfinders, and more).

Therefore, if librarians are a special class of question answerers, and digital reference is a special class of question answering (one that involves an information professional indoctrinated into the practice, theory, ethics, and principles of librarianship), is there any reason to wonder whether this special case should include more participatory aspects? Part of the answer may be seen in "social search." Social search (for examples, see Dalal, 2007; Yanbe et al., 2007) is the direct inclusion of

human expertise into improving search results. This might be utilizing folksonomies like tagging to refine search results, incorporation of social bookmarking into search results (Bao et al., 2007), even a service like Wikia that built a search engine from social tools like Wikis. In this lecture, I mentioned Reference Extract, a proposed search engine that builds search from the citation patterns of reference librarians. All of these examples begin to redefine the boundary of user and service, reference, and software. After all, if the divide between search engine and searcher can crumble, why not that between user and expert in a reference transaction?

Take, for example, the embedded librarian (Brown & Dean, 2007). In many contexts, from hospitals to research centers, information professionals have become part of teams. So librarians make the rounds with doctors so they are better able to understand questions and to proactively provide information to doctors (Brown, 2004). During a research trip to the U.S. Department of Justice, several lawyers talked about how legal librarians are not just becoming part of litigation teams, they are increasingly being treated as investigators gathering facts and identifying expert witnesses on key cases. There is still a divide between the ultimate end user (in this case, doctors and lawyers) and the library, but the embedded librarians act as a bridge with feet in both contexts.

To further answer the question of what a truly participatory reference might look like, I worked with OCLC's QuestionPoint team to reimagine digital reference software from a participatory perspective. The new software would need to:

- Put the user in control
- Allow the user to not simply collect information, but to organize the information in a relational manor (like an entailment mesh)
- Allow the user to determine the conversants
- Promote back and forth exchanges

The result is a conceptual system called "scapes."

5.1   SCAPES

Think of a big digital "table." As you find a site, you place it on the table. You find a good book—on the table. An e-mail from a friend goes on the table too. As you get a better idea of what is going on, you begin to make piles. Like items, say the same approach to getting a child into a sleeping routine, go into a pile together. You can also draw lines between the objects and add notes to the lines like "these sources agree," or "this person is so wrong." All the time you are moving and sorting objects, the "table" is recording and watching so you can play back how you arrived at a given point, or rewind to a previous state. The table is also suggesting new items that might help you based on how others organized these items. You can also invite other people to join you at the table. They

are able to see your organization and also, if you let them, add and change the structure. Maybe you invite a librarian to work on your table, or a friend, or a professor.

Once you have completed your table, you can make it available for anyone else to see and use for their own information problem. Just as you linked books and e-mails on your table, someone can link in your entire table, building upon it and making an instantly visible representation of knowledge.

This is the idea behind scapes. Scapes will be a piece of web-hosted software and allied services that support the building of these tables, or scapes (like "landscape" or "mindscape"). It is intended to provide an efficient and effective means of representing ideas and knowledge as a series of connected facts, objects, observations, and ideas. It provides the opportunity to visually build knowledge in a computationally intelligible way. It is akin to concept mapping the reader may be familiar with, but not limited to a single "root" concept. They are also more dynamic, include a more complex linking of items, and are geared towards aggregation across different concepts.

Figure 5.1 shows the primary interface to create a "scape." This interface is sure to evolve as the project progresses and through direct user input.

The interface is deliberately sparse, just like the empty table from the above scenario. This sparse interface and limited tools allow users to organize their materials in their own fashion, not confined by some preexisting organizational scheme. The three tools in the top right are simply "add objects," "talk to a person," and "search." The functions of these buttons will become obvious soon.

In this set of screens, a man named John was driving home from work one day listening to the radio and heard the song "Rich Girl" by Gwen Stefani. John thought he had heard a song like that

FIGURE 5.1: Primary interface to create a scape.

FIGURE 5.2:

before, but could not remember where. Arriving home, he went to his library online and started a scape on the subject. The first thing John did was a simple search on "rich girl" (Figure 5.2).

It is a basic search so it brings up a lot of results. John finds the song at the bottom of the list and drags it into the scape. A simple click on the song would play it and show standard bibliographic data like that stored in catalogs. With a click, he can make a standing link between the song and the album it came from (Figure 5.3).

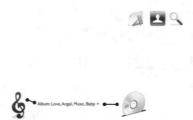

FIGURE 5.3:

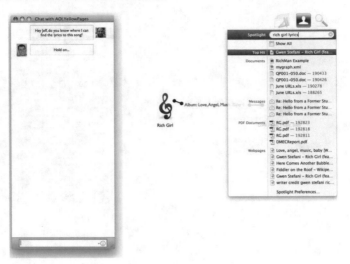

FIGURE 5.4:

This does not really tell John what he is interested in—is it a remake?—so he brings in a friend to help think about this. John uses the second button in the upper right corner of the screen and adds a chat session with his friend Jeff. John asks Jeff if he knows where to find the lyrics to the song. Jeff does a search (using the same tools available to John—as seen in Figure 5.4), and finds that someone has already created a public scape on the lyrics to this song.

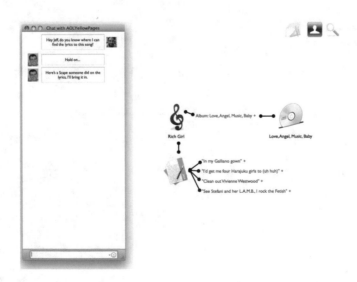

FIGURE 5.5:

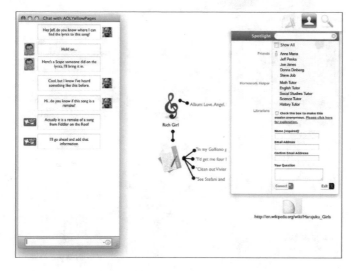

FIGURE 5.6:

Jeff drags the existing object into John's workspace. Because this is not a simple text file but another scape, meaning a complete workspace with relationships and context, John gets not only the lyrics but the links someone has made between parts of the lyrics and additional information. In this case, this added scape includes four threads based on the lyrics (as seen in the lower right portion of Figure 5.5).

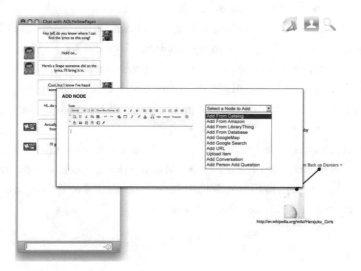

FIGURE 5.7:

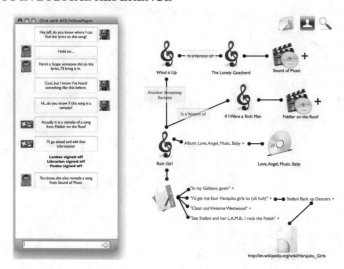

FIGURE 5.8:

Following one of the threads, "I'd get me four Harajuku girls to (uh huh)" John can find out that Harajuku girls are Gwen Stefani's back up dancers, and even a link to Wikipedia to see that they took their name from a fashionable subway stop in Tokyo.

Still, as interesting as this is, it is not helping John on his quest to find the origin of this song. John goes back to his "talk to a person" button and brings in a librarian. John then asks the librarian "Hi . . . do you know if this song is a remake?" to which the librarian replies, "Actually it is a remake of a song from Fiddler on the Roof" (Figure 5.6).

The librarian then uses the "add objects" button to bring up a window (visible and available to all and seen in Figure 5.7) and adds links to the original *Fiddler on the Roof* song "If I Were a Rich Man" and links that song to information on the musical soundtrack.

Happy with the results, all sign off. As this scape may be useful to others, John leaves it public so that others may see it (and include it), and John allows all the original participants to edit the scape whenever they want.

In fact, later that night, as Jeff is driving home, he hears another Gwen Stefani song "Start it Up," which contains elements from the Sound of Music. He logs back into the scape, and he adds that information as well (as seen in Figure 5.8). John will be alerted to the change through RSS and can always keep this document live or lock it down.

·   ·   ·   ·

CHAPTER 6

Conclusion

In a special issue of *Reference & User Services Quarterly*, I wrote (with the conviction that only comes from youth):

> Let us not, however, look at digital reference in its early stages and claim that is either unused or that we have seen the medium's full potential. Reference and reference librarians must continue to evolve. With additional tools, technology and experience, digital reference processes will become increasingly manageable and efficient, and will minimize the workloads of already busy library staff. Readers of this issue should heed the cries of an infant digital reference field, or they will be deafened by the roars of the coming reference revolution.

While the reference revolution might not have been a deafening roar, it was (and is) very real. When digital reference started, it did so in an environment where the scholarship, practice, and publications of the field were filled with discussion of things. Articles on reference were almost always about reference resources. Reference courses in higher education were all about genres (what is an atlas? what is a gazetteer? when would you use an encyclopedia?). The bulk of intermediation research in reference was 20 years old and seemed frozen after Hernon and McClure's 55% rule and Dervin's neutral questioning. Today, after the "revolution," reference is about people again. Reference has become a valued conversation and not simply a band-aid to bad information systems.

Arm's mortal in the portal did not just roll over and die, but it stood waiting as the users ran over the gates of elite-controlled collections. As users abandoned elite authority web sites for participatory systems that made the user part of the system, reference as a system decision began to shine. Collections form questions, human expertise incorporated directly into systems, and increasingly a social approach to knowledge have moved reference from the periphery of the digital library to the center. In that progression, however, reference itself has begun to change. No longer can digital reference be defined as an expert passively waiting for a single user's questions. Now reference must become a facilitated social process centered on knowledge, not things.

· · · · ·

Acknowledgments

The author would like to acknowledge Gary Marchionini and Diane D. Cerra for their patience and guidance in the creation of this lecture. Also due for special thanks are the participatory team at Syracuse for their help in forming the underlying particiaptory librarianship concept: Todd Marshall, David Pimental, Jaime Snyder, Keisuke Inhoue, Gabrielle Gosslin, Joanne Silverstein, Scott Nicholson, and Usha Ramnarine-Rieks. Thanks to the OCLC QuestionPoint team in helping to advance participatory concepts into the area of reference. One last note of thanks must go out to the number of reference librarians who generously provided their insight and comments into the advancement of participatory librarianship and participatory reference.

References

Abels, E. (1996). The e-mail reference interview. *RQ*, 35:345–358.

Arms, W. (2002). The National Science Digital Library as an example of information science research. *OCLC Distinguished Speakers Series*. Retrieved from http://www.oclc.org/programsandresearch/dss/ppt/dss_arms.ppt.

Bao, S., Xue, G., Wu, X., Yu, Y., Fei, B., & Su, Z. (2007). Optimizing web search using social annotations. *WWW '07: Proceedings of the 16th International Conference on World Wide Web*. New York: ACM. doi:10.1145/1242572.1242640

Belkin, N. J. (1980). Anomalous states of knowledge as a basis for information retrieval. *Canadian Journal of Information Science*, *5*, 133–143.

Bertland, L. H. (1986). An overview of research in metacognition: Implications for information skills instruction. *School Library Media Quarterly*, *15*, 96–99.

Brown, H. (2004). Clinical medical librarian to clinical informationist. *Reference Services Review*, *32*(1), 45–49. doi:10.1108/00907320410519397

Brown, D., & Leith, D. (2007). Integration of the research library service into the editorial process: "Embedding" the librarian into the media. *Aslib Proceedings*, *59*(6), 539–549. doi:10.1108/00 012530710839614

Bry, L (2000). Simple and sophisticated methods for processing large volumes of question and answer information through the World Wide Web. In Lankes, R. D., Collins, J., & Kasowitz, A. S. (Eds.), *Digital reference services in the new millennium*. New York: Neal-Schuman.

Carter, D. S., & Janes, J. (2000). Unobtrusive data analysis of digital reference questions and service at the Internet public library: An exploratory study. *Library Trends*, *49*(2), 251–265.

Dalal, M. (2007). Personalized social & real-time collaborative search. *WWW '07: Proceedings of the 16th international Conference on World Wide Web*. New York: ACM. doi:10.1145/1242572.12 42810

Dervin, B., & Dewdney, P. (1986). Neutral questioning: A new approach to the reference interview. *RQ*, *25*, 506–513.

Durrance, J. C. (1989). Reference success: Does the 55 percent rule tell the whole story? *Library Journal*, *114*(7), 31–36.

Hernon, P., & McClure, C. R. (1987). *Unobtrusive testing and library reference services*. Norwood: Ablex.

Kaske, N., & Arnold, J. (2005). Evaluating the quality of a chat service. *Portal: Libraries and the Academy*, *5*(2), 177–193. doi:10.1353/pla.2005.0017

Kibbee, W., & Ma, I. J. L. (2004). Do virtual reference librarians dream of digital reference questions? A qualitative and quantitative analysis of e-mail and chat reference. *Australian Academic & Research Libraries*, *35*(2), 95–110.

Lankes, R. D. (1998). *Building & maintaining internet information services: K-12 digital reference services*. Syracuse: ERIC Clearinghouse on Information & Technology.

Lankes, R. D., Goodrum, A., & Nicholson, S. (Eds.). (2003). *The digital reference research agenda. Publications in librarianship*. Chicago: Association of College & Research Libraries.

McClure, C., Lankes, R. D., Gross, M., & Choltco-Devlin, B. (2002). *Statistics, measures and quality standards for assessing digital reference library services: Guidelines and procedures*. Syracuse: ERIC Clearinghouse on Information & Technology.

Miwa, M. (2000). *Use of human intermediation in information problem solving: A users' perspective*. Dissertation, Syracuse University School of Information Studies.

Mon, L. (2006). *User perceptions of digital reference services*. Ph.D. dissertation, University of Washington.

Mon, L., & Janes, J. (2007). The thank you study: User feedback in e-mail 'thank you' messages. *Reference and User Services Quarterly*, *46*(4), 53–59.

Nicholson, S., & Lankes, R. D. (2007). The Digital Reference Electronic Warehouse (DREW) Project: Creating the infrastructure for digital reference research through a multi-disciplinary knowledge base. *Reference and User Services Quarterly*, *46*(3), 45–59.

Nilsen, K. (2005). Virtual versus face-to-face reference: Comparing users' perspectives on visits to physical and virtual reference desks in public and academic libraries. Retrieved from http://www.ifla.org/IV/ifla71/papers/027e-Nilsen.pdf.

OCLC (2007). What is virtual reference? Retrieved September 26, 2007, from http://www.oclc.org/questionpoint/about/virtual/default.htm.

Pask, G. (1976). *Conversation theory: applications in education and epistemology*. New York: Elsevier.

Pomerantz, J. (2003). Integrating digital reference service into the digital library environment. In Lankes, R. D., Goodrum, A., & Nicholson, S. (Eds.), *The digital reference research agenda. Publications in librarianship*. Chicago: Association of College & Research Libraries.

Pomerantz, J., & Silverstein, J. (2003). Creating a system for shared information and referral: The importance of ontology. In Lankes, R. D., McClure, C., Gross, M., & Pomerantz, J. (Eds.), *In implementing digital reference services: Setting standards and making it real*. New York: Neal-Schuman.

Pomerantz, J., Mon, L., & McClure, C. R. (2008). Evaluating remote reference service: A practical guide to problems and solutions. *Portal: Libraries and the Academy*, *8*(1), 15–30.

Pomerantz, J., Nicholson, S., Belanger, Y., & Lankes, R. D. (2004). The current state of digital reference: Validation of a general digital reference model through a survey of digital reference services. *Information Processing & Management*, *40*(2), 347–363. doi:10.1016/S0306-4573(02)00085-7

Radford, M. L. (2001). Encountering users: Applying interpersonal communication theory in the library context. *Journal of Education for Library and Information Science*, *42*(1), 27–41.

Radford, M. L., & Connaway, L. S. (2007). "Screenagers" and live chat reference: Living up to the promise. *Scan*, *26*(1), 31–39.

Richardson, J. V., Jr. (1999). Understanding the reference transaction: A systems analysis perspective. *College & Research Libraries*, *60*(3), 211–222.

Ruppel, M., & Fagan, J. C. (2002). Instant messaging reference: Users' evaluation of library chat. *Reference Services Review*, *30*(3), 183–197. doi:10.1108/00907320210435464

RUSA (2004). Guidelines for implementing and maintaining virtual reference services. Retrieved September 26, 2007, from http://www.ala.org/ala/rusa/rusaprotools/referenceguide/virtrefguidelines.htm.

Saxton, M., & Richardson, J. (2002). *Understanding reference transactions: Transforming an art into a science*. New York: Academic Press.

Shachaf, P., & Horowitz, S. (2006). Are virtual reference services color blind? *Library & Information Science Research*, *28*(4), 501–520. doi:10.1016/j.lisr.2006.08.009

Shachaf, P., Meho, L. I., & Hara, N. (2007). Cross-cultural analysis of virtual reference. *The Journal of Academic Librarianship*, *33*(2), 243–253.

Southwick, S. B. (2001). *Understanding intermediation in a digital environment: An exploratory case study*. Dissertation, Syracuse University.

Taylor, R. (1968). Question negotiation and information seeking in libraries. *College & Research Libraries*, *29*, 178–194.

Ward, D. (2003). Using virtual reference transcripts for staff training. *Reference Services Review*, *31*(1), 46–56. doi:10.1108/00907320310460915

Yanbe, Y., Jatowt, A., Nakamura, S., & Tanaka, K. (2007). Can social bookmarking enhance search in the web? *JCDL '07: Proceedings of the 7th ACM/IEEE-CS Joint Conference on Digital Libraries*. New York: ACM. doi:10.1145/1255175.1255198

Author Biography

R. David Lankes is director of the Information Institute of Syracuse and an associate professor in Syracuse University's School of Information Studies. Lankes has always been interested in combining theory and practice to create active research projects that make a difference. Past projects include the ERIC Clearinghouse on Information and Technology, the Gateway to Education Materials, AskERIC, and the Virtual Reference Desk. Lankes' more recent work involves how participatory concepts can reshape libraries and credibility. This work expands his ongoing work to understand the integration of human expertise in information systems. Lankes is a passionate advocate for libraries and their essential role in today's society. He also seeks to understand how information approaches and technologies can be used to transform industries. In this capacity, he has served on advisory boards and study teams in the fields of libraries, telecommunications, education, and transportation, including at the National Academies. He has been appointed as a visiting fellow at the National Library of Canada, the Harvard School of Education, and the first fellow of American Library Association's Office for Information Technology Policy.